MY JOURNEY TO IRONMAN

Endurance Sports as a Means of Individuation

Copyright ©2020 ANALYTICAL PSYCHOLOGY PRESS

All rights reserved. No part of this publication may be reproduced, distributed, or transmitted in any form or by any means, including photocopying, recording, or other electronic or mechanical methods, without the prior written permission of the publisher, except in the case of brief quotations embodied in critical reviews and certain other noncommercial uses permitted by copyright law. For permission requests, write to the publisher, addressed "Attention: Permissions Coordinator," at orders@analyticalpsychologypress.com

ANALYTICAL PSYCHOLOGY PRESS
280 Elm Street, Oberlin, OH 44074-1504, United States
https://analyticalpsychologypress.com
Editor and Publisher: Dyane Sherwood

ORDERING INFORMATION
ItascaBooks - orders@itascabooks.com - manages direct orders and distribution to individuals, groups, libraries, retail stores, and online book sellers.
Telephone Orders: +1 800 901 3480, ext. 118 (9am-5pm Central US Time Zone) or FAX: 1-952-920-0541.
Quantity Sales: Special discounts are available on quantity purchases by groups, associations, and others. For details, contact: orders@itascabooks.com

https://analyticalpsychologypress.com
My Journey to Ironman: Endurance Sports as a Means of Individuation/ Warren W. Sibilla Jr. —1st ed.
ISBN: 978-1-7346582-4-8

MY JOURNEY TO IRONMAN

Endurance Sports as a Means of Individuation

Warren W. Sibilla Jr.

ANALYTICAL PSYCHOLOGY PRESS
Oberlin, Ohio, United States of America

Reviews

Dr. Warren Sibilla's book, *My Journey to Ironman: Endurance Sports as a Means of Individuation*, follows in the Jungian tradition, which demonstrates that it is in the particular that we find the universal. He shows the reader that, through scrupulous reflection on the personal details of one's life, there emerges the awareness and appreciation of the deepest archetypal truths of the human psyche. Writing with an honest, clear, and joyous voice, Dr. Sibilla invites the reader to accompany him on his quest for wholeness and challenges us to endure our own journeys with consciousness and humility.

—Kenneth W. James, Ph.D, Diplomate Jungian Analyst

In his dramatic account of both physical and psychological transformation, Warren Sibilla takes the reader on a journey through dreams and relentless training culminating in his successful completion of the Ironman competition. Sibilla's insightful response to his dreams and their incorporation into consciousness is a model of the analytic process, and it is not surprising that as he builds on his training for competition, he finds his clinical process changing as well. For an account of how psyche can express itself through athletic competition leading to deep personal growth, this book is highly recommended.

—George Hogenson, Ph.D. Jungian Analyst

Jung's concept of the individuation process provides us with a helpful psychological reference or frame to finding meaning and leading a fulfilling life. This process, which unfolds over a lifetime, includes establishing one's identity in the first half of life and then at midlife brings a change in one's focus to align with more interior and personal values. Jung's terminology and use of arcane symbolism such as the alchemical process to explain this process can make it sometimes rather difficult to fully grasp and comprehend.

In his book, *My Journey to Ironman: Endurance Sports as a Means of Individuation*, Warren Sibilla manages what can only be described as an heroic accomplishment in providing the reader with a grounded, accessible, and realistic example of what a phase in this process can look like in everyday life. By openly sharing with the reader his personal struggle in coming to terms with uncertainty and the need to find direction at a certain point in his life, the author bares his soul as he is forced to confront doubt and the struggle to find his bearings in his early forties. While the journey undertaken eventually leads the author to participate in an Ironman event, the focus of this book is on the inner process and the evolving ability of the author to trust his instincts, to rely on dream images to guide him, and to rely on the helpful figures who present themselves along his path, that make this book such a captivating read. The author's frank, forthright, and intimate recounting of his journey, without the slightest hint of exhibitionism or narcissistic grandiosity, manages to make his journey emotionally palpable and provides the reader with a realistic, touching, and deeply moving account.

Individuation is a never-ending process. It is about becoming deeply involved in life in a manner that reflects the uniqueness of who we really are. This book stands out as an example of this process, of what it demands of us, but also of the gifts it can offer. I highly recommend this book without reservation and am confident it will be of great benefit to the reader and will leave no reader unmoved.

—Tom Kelly

This is a story of a profound Jungian Analyst and of an ardent athlete, and how they are one and the same. There is no dividing line in Warren Sibilla. Writing with immediacy, Warren brings us with him to the indivisablity of body and psyche—the psychoid. His breath-soul runs, swims, and bikes into unity with all of nature and, yes, with the Divine. Prescient wisdom from the Dream World joins Waking World happenings in knock-your-socks-off synchronicities, making the reality and the grace of the Unknown undeniable. All the while, Warren is held by the love of his family, the fathering-forth of Greg, his trainer, and *participation mystique* with fellow athletes. Even the reader who never ran around the block will find stories that kindle dedication to her own individuation. One such story for me is the time Warren sacrificed following a marathon pacer, daring to trust his own internal pacing rhythm. At the finish line, he was embraced by a grateful first-time marathoner who, unbeknownst to Warren, had been following him for ten miles. "I couldn't have done it without you," the younger man said. Warren had *become* a pacer, an elder.

It could be said of Warren that he has fought the good fight, he has finished the course, he has kept the faith. Except, of course, he is continuing to do so in whatever way he is called.

—**Donnamarie Flanagan**

Dedications

To my wife, Maureen. Maureen has been my biggest supporter and never wavered no matter the challenge in front of us- not once. I very fondly recall the countless times she drove to a halfway point on a long bike ride to provide me with fresh water bottles, some calories to finish the training, and a loving word of encouragement. I also recall with gratitude the many times she drove the SAG (supplies and gear) vehicle on my 100 mile rides—driving just far enough ahead of me to help ensure no dangerous dogs (we call them runners as compared to the barkers marking their territory) and to push me a bit further before stopping to allow me to fill up for the next stint. If I had a nickel for every time Maureen has heard me say, "You know, I am really sore tonight," we would be wealthy. On the contrary, ours is a different kind of wealth. She, for her part, has repeatedly asked me, "I don't know how you do it- how do you do that?" The answer to that question is easy, "Your love sustains me no matter what." Thank you.

To my four children. We often did not have traditional vacations. Instead, we traveled throughout the country with wonderful comraderies called athletes and triathletes. We supported one another as we raced and watched as our children grew up together. My children often accompanied me riding a bike during my long runs carrying fresh water and extra calories for which I am forever grateful. One of the ways that I endured the long swims, in addition to reflection and meditation on my dreams, was to divide the total laps by four, the number of our children, and for each of those intervals, I would remind myself of all the grace and splendor of each child ending with a prayer for their safety and wellbeing. Thank you.

To each and every one of my teachers. It is said that among Michelangelo's last words were, "I am still learning." I have learned through long distance endurance sports that much is accomplished, on the course and off, by maintaining a "beginner's mind" of awe and wonder- letting every "thing" teach me something. I remain in the debt of each of my teachers. Thank you.

The Collected Works of C. G. Jung are cited in form of volume and paragraph number: CW X, ¶X Multiple paragraphs are indicated by double paragraph symbols: CW X, ¶¶X-XX.

Table of Contents

Prologue	xiii
Chapter 1: My Journey Begins with a Dream	1
Chapter 2: Something's Not Right	7
Chapter 3: Breath is the Teacher	15
Chapter 4: One of Many	23
Chapter 5: Dream Trophy	35
Chapter 6: *Spiritus Rector*	53
Chapter 7: The Transcendent Function	59
Chapter 8: A Symbol of Renewal	63
Epilogue	69
References	73
Index	75
About the Author	78

Prologue

THIS is a book about the otherworldly magic and intrigue of dreams and their unfolding in everyday life. The ancient Sybils (Latin *Sibylla*), from which my last name is derived, were said to be female priests who, in one manner or another, spent their days divining the future such as by interpreting dreams. Also, my mother reminded me that my first book report I wrote in the third grade was on a book about dreams and that I had a practice of asking my siblings about their dreams at the morning breakfast table. Thus, it could be said that I have been interested in dreams for a very long time. I decided to study psychology in college and the second course I took after the mandatory Introduction to Psychology class, was a class on personality theory. I distinctly recall during the first week that the professor talked about Sigmund Freud after discussing the plan for the semester and the requirements for the course. However, the second week, he presented the theory of Analytical Psychology and C. G. Jung's primary emphasis on the mythopoetic nature of the psyche—the story-telling nature of our being and the chief means of the story being the nature of the dream. This was one of those experiences where I was completely immersed in the material, so much so that the professor took notice and commented upon my demeanor after the class ended. He asked if I wanted to join the local Friends of Jung group that met nearby periodically to listen to a lecture by a Jungian analyst and then discuss the ideas afterward. He indicated that I could join as a student member. I did join and quickly realized that indeed, I wanted to eventually train to become a Jungian Psychoanalyst.

I mentioned my intention to my professor advisor who encouraged me to pursue such advanced training but only after first completing my Ph.D., advice that I still treasure to this day. Training to become a Jungian Psychoanalyst involves first going through a series of interviews and if deemed appropriate for the advanced nature of the training, one is formally admitted to a training institute—where, at the end of each year of study, one is provided with the opportunity for continued discernment by way of oversight committee meetings. The formal training includes no less than four years of academic coursework, participation in one's own weekly psychoanalysis and weekly supervision of one's professional work. Typically, after two or three years of coursework, there is a series of written and oral examinations over the breadth of Jung's thought that tests the candidate's knowledge and application of the material. Once these examinations are successfully completed, the candidate moves to the advanced level of training and begins accruing hours toward sitting for the two final examinations. These accrued hours include one's own continuing weekly psychoanalysis as well as the hours associated with continued supervision of one's work. Typically, this next phase of training is completed in no less than two years. When the necessary hours have been accrued, the candidate is invited to complete a thesis and present two cases of patients they have been seeing in their clinical practice. This results in two final oral examinations, which, when successfully completed, earn the candidate the Diploma in Analytic Psychology and the professional designation of Psychoanalyst—the highest level of training for professionals who provide advanced psychotherapy.

This book is the culmination of many years of dedication to the study and application of Jung's theories of psychological functioning and offers the reader a window into the process of one individual grappling with what Jung termed, "Individuation." That is, a view of the process of coming to realize and live out one's purpose and meaning to the fullest extent possible and thereby, give expression to the unfolding of what Jung eventually came to call the "Self." This book accomplishes this feat by way of sharing intimate details of dreams, their practical application, the humorous and heroic sides of life, and always the fantastical linking power of imagination.

To see a World in a grain of Sand
And a Heaven in a Wildflower
Hold Infinity in the palm of your hand
And Eternity in an hour
                —William Blake

For the unconscious is not this thing or that; it is the Unknown as it immediately affects us.
                —C. G. Jung

The kingdom is inside of you and it is outside of you. When you come to know yourselves, then you will become known.
                —Gnostic Gospel of Thomas

Chapter 1

My Journey Begins with a Dream

Several nights before I was to run in the Detroit Marathon, I had the following dream:

> *I was out swimming with three other people—two women and one man all of whom I did not know but felt very comfortable with. We were way out in the middle of a body of water—a huge lake. Above us was beautiful blue sky accompanied by a very warm, large, yellow sun. I asked the woman: "How far do you think it is to over there? (I pointed to a small island). She answered, "That is one-half mile." I said in reply, "That's perfect, I know I can do that!" I was so excited and felt so full of potential. I began swimming and soon felt myself to be in a rhythm with the water, my body, my breath, and my feelings. I reached the island and began talking with the island people. They were so friendly and welcoming. I explained that I had just swum from over there to here. A woman then said to me (while pointing toward the water), "The key is to always use your breath as your guide; breathe deeply and purposely."*

At this point the dream shifts:

> *I am with an older woman and we were way out in the water—so far out that land was not in sight. Beneath us was a sunken ship with treasure inside. I asked if she wanted to go down and explore it. She was hesitant, waiting for me and my reply. I said, "Well I am going." She replied, "OK, good, I will go with you." We went down, deep down into the water. Soon we arrived at the ship and went inside. I realized quickly that within the ship there was air and I could breathe fine. We began exploring and I moved my arms and hands back and forth across the bottom of the boat's hull. I uncovered a treasure and looked at my female guide who was watching me throughout this whole process. She simply smiled at me and I woke up with a very warm feeling.*

At the marathon's starting line, I was utterly and completely terrified; so scared in fact, that I was noticeably shaking and could hardly breathe. My dream was very far from my mind. I thought of quitting before I even began—more than once. There is no shame in just walking back to the hotel room—I tried to imagine leaving the start line, sneaking away and just could not do it. A look to my wife who was waiting for the start on the sidewalk and my tears began to flow—quitting was not a possibility. So why was I doing this? I did not look like a runner and certainly did not feel like a runner. I had trained to lose weight—or so I thought. I had trained to help manage stress I reasoned. I had trained to…I really did not know why I was there. But I was at the start line of a marathon. It was cold, so dark I could hardly see, and I was surrounded by several thousand people I did not know in the very early morning hours. Amidst my swirling, disorienting anxiety I vaguely recalled the National Anthem being sung and my next memory was the starting gun going off. Instinctively I began to put one foot in front of the other and began the marathon shuffle making my way to the starting line. Across the tape and I was off on my marathon journey.

Within a few miles the mass of runners had thinned such that I had room to move my arms freely and I could see around me in all directions. I felt completely alone, and my anxiety only increased. I could not get these incessant questions out of my mind: "Why was I doing this?" and "Why am I here?" Even so, I tried to settle myself down enough to focus on the task at hand. Over the Ambassador Bridge, into Canada for several miles—through the underground tunnel and back into Detroit my legs were growing very heavy and I began feeling more tired than scared. We made our way out across the Freedom Bridge onto Belle Isle to mark the halfway point of the marathon. I took notice of the day; the darkness of the morning was gone, the sun was out and very bright, and the wind was crisp, consistent with a fall marathon.

Half-way around Belle Isle I found myself in a group of six or eight runners. Trying to distract my mind from the mounting pain and fatigue, I was listening to the conversation of the other runners. Their talk centered on their favorite foods and what they were going to treat themselves with after the race. I said to the woman next to me, "I am really tired. I wish I had my music with me right now—that would really help me to feel better." She looked at me directly and replied, "No, that is not what you need. Listen to me, all you need to do is breathe deeply—breathe into yourself and follow your breath—this will give you everything you need. Just focus on your breath."

I was so taken by what this woman had said to me that I felt completely and entirely removed from our conversation. When I came back to the moment, I saw that she was gone, and I felt alone again. Recalling her advice to focus on my breathing, I instantly remembered my dream from the previous night and the instructions I received from my female dream companion, "*The key is to always use your breath as your guide; breathe deeply and purposely.*" I was filled absolutely with a warm spirit and felt a profound connection to my body and my deepest emotions. Tears began to flow as I asked myself many, many times over the next miles on Belle Isle, "Was she really there? Did I hear her? Or did I hallucinate her?" "This is not a coincidence, is it?" Then I thought to myself, "I crossed the Freedom Bridge and felt heavy from my anxiety and worry; I communicated my feeling to the woman next to me with my personal solution to my situation; and she corrected me placing the emphasis on my breath. Soon, I will be going back over the same Freedom Bridge, but I certainly feel very different!"

My questions notwithstanding, I felt carried along for the second half of the marathon with a completely new awareness and energy. That is, no matter what message my mind sent my way regarding quitting and not finishing or my body pain and fatigue, I was able to draw on this new awareness and receive renewed strength. It was as if I was being carried along, a feeling and experience I had never felt before.

With one mile to go, I knew I would finish. I began crying so hard I could not run but only managed a fast walk—it was not about running anymore or even completing my first marathon. The miles, the early morning runs, the sacrifices made regarding my diet, all of the aching, tired muscles at the end of the day—everything seemed so incredibly purposeful. All my training memories were flooding me, and I felt so fully that the sacrifices made during my training were now meaningful and purposeful. I was doing exactly and completely what I was supposed to be doing then and there in that moment. It was the most soul-filled occurrence I had ever experienced in athletics. I simply wanted to drink down every moment of it on the streets of downtown Detroit and I slowed to be certain I did not miss a drop.

I looked up in the sky—the sun still shining brightly and said my prayer of thanksgiving. When I looked back at the road in front of me a large man had joined me from the crowded sidewalk. He hugged me and said, "That is so cool man—just keep going up around the corner and you are finished!" With that he let go of me and I was through the finisher's shoot. I met up with my wife and amidst my tears all I could say was, "I did it." From this point forward, I was aware of a source, a center, an energy within me that I had experienced on Belle Isle and that I was fully in relationship with. That is, I was keenly and unmistakably aware that it was anything but "*me*" that "*did it*" but I struggled to name "*it*"—in fact, words seemed completely secondary and in some essential way, even to spoil my experience. This is an example of what Jung pointed toward when he said that to truly understand the archetype it must be experienced as an autonomous energy that serves to reshape one's entire life (CW 7 ¶184).

In the weeks that followed my first marathon experience, I reflected on what had happened to me. The same warm feelings I felt on Belle Isle continued to carry me along as I physically recovered from the marathon. The first time I reentered the health club where I trained for so many hours, all I could do was cry tears of gratitude. It was clear that I had experienced a numinous event.

The experience of the numinous is a clarion call to learn about and experience the psyche by trusting the inner intuition and thereby immersing oneself in all aspects of life. It is there, in the so-called incidental events of one's life, that the psyche reveals itself to those able to apprehend the experience. Consciously, I trained for and ran the Detroit marathon for very personal reasons: to lose weight, to manage my daily stress, and to challenge myself physically—all far removed from my analytic training. In fact, I thought I was seeking an avenue of release/escape far from analytic training. Instead, I experienced a depth of the psyche not possible for me otherwise.

In documenting the journey of the hero in his famous book, Joseph Campbell wrote that the first task of the hero is to retreat from the world, from the usual and customary, and to attempt something extraordinary, to "break through to the undistorted…experience of the archetypal images." Campbell continued, "The second solemn task and deed is to return transfigured and teach the lesson he has learned of his life renewed" (Campbell, 1949). To this end, this book is about how my training for and competing in long distance endurance athletics served as a means of informing my individuation—Jung's grand concept for the unfolding of one's psychological maturity. This book will link Jung's theory of the transcendent function focusing on the role of dreams, fantasy and symbols, development of the inferior function, and elucidation of the archetype with training for and competing in long distance endurance sports. In so doing, the reader will explore in what ways my training for and competing in endurance sports has served as what Jung termed, a personal *spiritus rector* informing my individuation.

Chapter 2

Something's Not Right

My isle people water dream came at a particularly frustrating and difficult time in my life. I was graduated into the control stage of analytic training and over the ensuing 12 to 18 months prior to my dream, I experienced two training cases drop out of treatment with me. I felt very lost and questioned my skills and abilities as an analyst-in-training. I struggled through several committee oversight meetings, one in particular when discussing my colloquium regarding the training cases that had dropped out of treatment. I was defensive and ultimately left the meeting feeling defeated and again, very lost. I simply could not feel any of the enthusiasm that led me to pursue the training to become a psychoanalyst.

While I could recall and, in fact, often thought about many of the fundamental dreams I had that seemed to encourage my seeking analytic training, many of my training experiences appeared to tell me otherwise. After consulting with several analysts, I took a leave of absence. I reasoned that the most honest action I could take would be to step away, put some distance between myself and my analytic training, allow the psyche to speak, and pray that I would be awake enough to hear it.

I recall saying to my monitoring committee in the meeting when I requested my leave, "I feel like I am forcing a square peg into a round hole—it just does not fit. It does not feel honest and I cannot, in good conscience, continue my training in this way. It just is not right." I was granted a leave of absence for one year, and I felt very alone leaving the building after the meeting. I cried most of the way home. Further, I promised myself that to be truly honest with the spirit of my leave of absence, I had to give every consideration to leaving the program entirely. I began imaging life without analytic training and without becoming an analyst.

In discussing the precondition for the operation of the transcendent function, Jung wrote,

> For this collaboration of opposing states to be possible at all, they must first face one another in the fullest conscious opposition. This necessarily entails a violent disunion with oneself, to the point where thesis and antithesis negate one another, while the ego is forced to acknowledge its absolute participation in both (CW 6 ¶824).

In this manner, I left the committee meeting with no conscious sense of direction or purpose—only to take a break and see where I ended up. In hindsight, it appears quite clear that my unconscious was preparing me for an experience that would dramatically expand my experience of psyche, far more comprehensive than was possible for me otherwise, and so powerful, in fact, as to significantly shape my individuation for many, many years to come. I was thinking the unthinkable, beginning to plan for a professional life outside of analytic training, and sought out long distance endurance sports as a refuge from my grief—or so I thought.

Instead, my unconscious initiated a fantastic journey deep into my body as a means of teaching me by experience. Regarding this psychic movement, Jung (1976) wrote,

> When the great swing has taken an individual into the world of symbolic mysteries, nothing comes of it, nothing can come of it, unless it has been associated with the earth, unless it has happened when that individual was in the body...And so individuation can only take place if you first return to the body, to your earth, only then does it become true (473).

After taking my leave of absence from analytic training, I found myself feeling heavy, confused, disoriented, and particularly restless. I had been running for several months and in fact, had completed several long-distance events such as a 21K and a 25K race. However, following an intuition, I decided to sign up and train for a marathon. It is not clear to me why I signed up, but I just felt a very curious energy when I thought about running a marathon. Each time I went to a marathon sign-up web site I would feel this new excitement—in fact, it was the only deep enthusiasm that I felt during that period of distress.

Eventually, after studying many different marathons, I settled on the Detroit Marathon, reasoning in particular, that it was close to my birthday and I would run this event as a birthday present to myself. That is, I felt like I needed to do something specifically for me, especially with this being my 40th birthday. I nervously pushed enter on my computer and with that I was signed up and immediately began training.

Reflecting on My Dream

In addition to my personal context, my water dream deserves much more comprehensive symbolic amplification as well. First of all, several environmental items are noteworthy. The dream takes place under the watchful presence of a large, yellow sun. Numerous texts and references support the symbolism of the sun as a representation of the Divine, as an image of God, and the creative potential of the soul (cf., CW 20 ¶¶138-206 and ¶¶ 212-224). In Christian tradition, Christ is likened to the sun, especially in its daily cyclical aspect nurturing the earth and its inhabitants and, in this way, is a symbol of the hero's birth, death, rebirth and transformation (cf., *Herder Symbol Dictionary*, 186-188). Such an otherwise incidental part of the dream is a rather sublime element serving as an overarching leitmotif. The sun intimating that the teleology of the dream is one of death and rebirth, and further, that this transformation takes place under the watchful attendance of a Divine presence. Joseph Campbell lecturing on the role of symbolism and mythology stated that in the medieval world, the Divine presence was understood as a function of only three illuminations: the stars, fire, and the sun (Campbell, 1996).

In commenting on the role of the sun in the hero's journey, Jung wrote,

> The inner voice is the voice of a fuller life, of a wider more comprehensive consciousness. That is why, in mythology, the birth of the hero or the symbolic rebirth coincides with sunrise, for the growth of personality is synonymous with an increase of self-consciousness. For the same reason most heroes are characterized by solar attributes, and the moment of birth of their greater personality is known as illumination. (CW 17 ¶318)

Also, when considering the context of the dream, my age, my difficult experiences in analytic training, and the sun image, one would also need to be mindful of midlife evident in the zenith of the sun.

The dream also takes place far out "in a huge lake" with three other swimmers, equally sorted between two males and two females. Such an image of matched fours suggests the working

Chapter 2: Something's Not Right

of what Jung has termed the Self (cf., CW 11 ¶¶56-107 and ¶¶280-285, CW 9ii ¶¶347-421, CW 9i ¶¶713-718 and CW 13 ¶¶358-368).

The fact that my numinous experience took place between crossings on the Freedom Bridge, out on Belle Isle and in liminal space also serves to underscore the synchronistic importance of my experience and the workings of the Self.

Contextually, the dream accentuates the "lost-ness" of my feelings placing me in the middle of large bodies of water. The element of water (as opposed to earth, as an example) signifying the fluidness of affect and emotion, the feeling/valuing function of the psyche. This dream image is entirely different from my typology, that being introverted thinking and intuition. Similar to the sun, the element of water also underscores the experience of rebirth, renewal, transformation, possibilities, and spiritual fertility (cf., *Herder Symbol Dictionary*, 211).

In the dream, I pose a question to one of the women, "How far do you think it is to over there?" This is a pivotal moment. It signifies the challenge—the test. For instance, my feelings of being in harmony with the elements (e.g. the water, my physical body, my breath, and my emotions) clearly were antithetical to how I felt otherwise. In this way, the ½ mile distance signified some ideal psychic distance necessary for change, transformation, growth and development. Contrary to my experiences in analytic training, in the dream I felt confident and stated I could accomplish that feat.

The isle people were very welcoming and possessed spiritual knowledge. After explaining my swimming accomplishment, I was told by one of the women, "The key is to always use your breath as your guide; breathe deeply and purposely." This wisdom would prove valuable and insightful beyond measure in the months and years to come. In this way, breath serves as a link to life, to meaning, to purpose—more specifically, breath as a metaphor for the transcendent function, a specific psychic bridge between conscious and unconscious (cf., CW 8 ¶¶131-193).

For example, in amplifying the image of breath, Jung linked one's breath with soul and Mercurius. Jung wrote, "As a 'subtle body' or 'breath soul' it means something non-material and finer than mere air. Its essential characteristic is to animate and be animated; it therefore represents the life principle" (CW 13 ¶262). Jung goes on to summarize the role of Mercurius thus:

> Mercurius consists of all conceivable opposites…He is both material and spiritual…He is the process by which the lower and material is transformed into the higher and spiritual…He is the devil, a redeeming psychopomp, an evasive trickster, and God's reflection in physical nature…He is also the reflection of a mystical experience…As such, he represents on the one hand the self and on the other the individuation process and, because of the limitless number of his names, also the collective unconscious. (CW 13 ¶284).

As a consequence, Mercurius was often identified as the Anima Mundi, the life animating principle.

In this regard, it should again be noted that my synchronistic experience of being reminded of using my breath occurred in the marathon at the half-way point. The zenith, the midpoint, is consistent with Jung's description of the transcendent function serving as a bridge between conscious and unconscious.

It should also not go unmentioned that the communicator of the essential breath message was a woman. And further, in the Detroit marathon I was reminded at the midpoint of the race, out on the isle between "here and there," in the liminal space that I was to use my breath as my guide, also by a woman. In this regard, Jung linked breath with *anima* saying, "Anima means soul…the soul is the magic breath of life, hence the term 'anima'" (CW 9i ¶55). Whether as many faceted Mercurius, a dream image, or the woman running next to me in the marathon, I am reminded to use my breath-*anima*-soul as my daily spiritual guide.

My dream then changes and I am taken out into the deep water again with this same life animating, breath-soul principle. After ensuring my participation, the two of us go down deep into a sunken ship with hidden treasure. My circumambulation of my arms signified the sacred ritual nature of our actions.

Finally, discovering the hidden treasure is consistent with the amplifications noted above as well as the mythological themes of the hero's high adventure (cf., Campbell, 1949). It is important to note that in the dream, the treasure is not to be possessed, only to be discovered and realized—to recognize one's breath-soul amongst the deep waters.

In summary then, the first part of my dream presents a rich and spirited environment under the watchful presence of Mercurius, an image of all conceivable opposites, or perhaps said differently, a wayfarer deity overseeing all possibilities—for example, Freedom's bridge. The setting is one of the hero's high adventure, in this instance learning to submit to one's breath as a means of spiritual knowing and relationship with a larger potential. Contrary to my conscious experience, the dream accentuates the fluidity of affect and emotion, in a word: animation, and further, links this animating feeling with a relationship with one's breath-soul. Also, in respect of teleos, it could be said that Mercurius is facilitating my transition into midlife.

The second half of the dream seems to underscore many of the themes from the first half with an emphasis on the collaborative role of the *anima* as well as *anima* serving as a bridge to the Self. Such an image was certainly compensatory with my life at that time—I had lost all animation and enthusiasm and was entirely unsure of my direction, far out in the deep waters and not seeing any particular direction in mind. In addition, the second half of the dream also draws attention to the practice of seeking the treasure deep within through the use of ritual, reflection, and experience—as opposed to action, knowing, and possession. These characteristically feminine traits draw a critical distinction between my conscious and unconscious attitudes at that time and thereby, again draw attention to the likely workings of the transcendent function as well as the Self.

In other words, the second part of the dream seems to declare: In order to discover the sacred meaning (ritual) in what you are doing, pay attention to your breath-soul, it will lead you to the treasure deep within. Further: note the ways in which this meaning making breath-soul operates in an environment of fluidity, without any hint of permanency or possession. And despite any worries to the contrary, learn how to find one's breath/life deep within this watery world. In this way, the dream points toward my need to be attentive to my feeling and sensation functions as well as the manner in which my thinking/intuitive functions squelch my experiences of the now—by seeking to possess the now and getting caught up in what might be around the corner.

In short then the compensatory function of the dream could be understood thus: with my thinking/intuitive functions in full tilt, I was placing the emphasis in my analytic work on product as opposed to experience, for example, becoming caught up in the number of analytic hours accrued, and thereby losing complete sight of the process. And when my analytic products were not being appreciated, I criticized the analyst-teachers instead of understanding my own inherent loss of process, experience, meaning, and the fluidity of the analytic relationship.

Chapter 3

Breath is the Teacher

AFTER running in the Detroit marathon, I continued my athletic training. With my body as my new analytic classroom and my breath-soul as teacher, I participated in many events, both locally and nationally. I grew to really enjoy the training and competing and continued to feel a purposeful connection to my athletic experiences. In an effort to broaden my training, I began cross-training by also swimming and bicycling and soon was signed up for my first triathlon.

Triathlons consist of three segments always in the same order: swim, bike and run and are generally organized around four traditional lengths. A sprint triathlon is generally comprised of a short swim of .25 to .5 mile swim (400 to 800 yards), 15 to 30 mile bicycle ride, and a 3 to 5 mile run. An Olympic distance (also known as the International distance) triathlon is comprised of a 1.5 kilometer swim (approximately one mile), a 40 kilometer bicycle ride (approximately 25 miles), and a 10 kilometer run (approximately 6 miles). A long-distance triathlon, also known as a Half-Ironman triathlon is comprised of a 1 ½ mile swim (2100 yards), a 56 mile bicycle ride, and a half-marathon run (21 kilometers; 13.1 miles). Finally, the Ironman triathlon is comprised of a 2.4 mile swim (4200 yards), a 112 mile bicycle ride, and a full marathon (42 kilometers or 26.2 miles). There is a fifth distance known as an "Ultra-Ironman" that is comprised of various distances of the three disciplines which, at a minimum, build upon the Ironman triathlon.

I entered my first triathlon, a sprint triathlon and began training. I used several computer-based training programs and was very excited to participate. The day came in early September and I awoke to very cold temperatures. Nonetheless, the race would go on. I parked my bike in my designated spot, laid out my running shoes and various accessories that I would need. Again, I was shaking I was so nervous. I had not done any open water swimming during my triathlon training and this event included a one-half mile lake swim.

My initial dream was again, very far from my mind. The gun went off and the open water swim start had begun. The swim start in a triathlon has aptly been described as "one attempting to swim in a blender." And so it was. I was pushed, kicked, and battered—in fact, I was kicked once in my gut so hard that I lost my breath. And second, at the half-way point of the swim where we rounded the turn buoy to begin heading back to shore, I was kicked in my forehead. After this kick, I "saw stars" and nearly passed out. I stopped, treaded water for a moment, and found myself next to one of the safety boats.

A safety worker asked me if I was alright. Not answering him, I again was asked if I was alright a few moments later. By this point, I was more aware of what had happened to me and I was terrified. I was out in the middle of the water and had to make a decision. Do I drop out and accept a ride in the boat back to the shore, or do I continue to swim and attempt to make it to the transition area? I decided to continue to swim. I struggled through the second half of the swim—both with physical pain, and with overwhelming anxiety. I exited the water in nearly last place. My wife met me on the shore and I simply looked at her in my terror. I had a living experience of my dream, being out in the middle of the lake and needing to tread water. I would need to connect to my breath-soul to have any chance of completing my first triathlon.

This being my first triathlon and not knowing the routine, I followed the lead of those athletes around me. I sat down by my bike, put my bike shoes and helmet on, and then I was off to complete the bike portion. I felt better as I went on and just wanted to forget the swim. I reasoned that I gave it my best shot, and maybe triathlons were not for me. "Just finish strong," I told myself. I completed the 18-mile bike portion and was so glad to put on my running shoes, the part of triathlon that I knew best—*terra firma*. I smiled more and more as I completed the five-mile run. Full of smiles and cheer as I crossed the finish line of my first triathlon, I was so glad to be done. As I reflected on my finish, I began to feel the same warm feelings that I felt during the Detroit marathon.

My initial triathlon experience proved pivotal. I felt as if my getting kicked in the head was what Joseph Campbell termed a threshold-liminal experience (cf., Campbell, 1949, 245). I again had a choice: to proceed forward despite my fear or to retreat to familiar ground. It was as if the unconscious was again putting the initial dream's meaning before me in an unmistakable manner: learn to connect with your breath-soul. If one does not constantly work to integrate the hard-won insight, the images and their symbols circle back around and find their way into one's life again! I knew (personally, experientially, and emotionally) my initial dream offered me solace regarding my swimming—still the experience of open water swimming terrified me.

After many months of internal debate, I decided to pursue another triathlon. However, this time I would not go at it alone. Instead, I would affiliate with like-minded individuals. I sought out and joined the local triathlon club. Preferably reserved and especially introverted, I consciously and purposely sought out the group's leadership and began volunteering to assist in various team-related tasks. My conscious intention was to honor my dream no matter my anxiety, submit to the opposites inherent in my dream, and jump in feet first. After the first year I was elected onto the Board of Directors where I was put in charge of membership and ordering our team uniforms. In addition, at the end of my first year, I was honored with a "Rookie of the Year" award at the annual team party—a plaque that I still have on my wall.

In addition, I hired a coach, Greg, a local professional triathlete that I was put into contact with. My relationship with Greg is so much more than a professional one. Joseph Campbell wrote, "For those who have not refused the call, the first encounter of the hero-journey is with a protective figure who provides the adventurer with amulets against the dragon forces he is about to pass" (Campbell, 1949, p. 69). And so it was. After many hours talking, Greg was to begin what was to become a treasured ritual: dispensing the weekly training schedule along with sage advice. That is, initially we would talk and discuss my goals, plans and work schedules, details about my body and fitness, family commitments, professional obligations. And then he would map out and write a training schedule consistent with the events I was training for sent to me in a weekly plan.

Receiving my weekly training schedule was to become what I experienced as a sacred ritual. That is, having honored my dream with my participation despite all of my anxieties, and having experienced the numinous in my events, I continually felt that my training and competing had become for me a daily means of putting myself in the presence of the sacred—my training schedule outlining my time with my Self. I could not wait to get to the pool and dive in. I treasured my time out on my bicycle. And running, my first love, continued to be a means of listening to my body and giving back through nutrition and attention, and thereby, honoring my breath-soul. As alone and directionless as I felt regarding my analytic training, I could clearly see that my endurance training was putting me in touch with a very special meaning and purpose and that my energies were continually leading me toward incredible experiences of psyche.

Regarding the dire need for soul-renewing ritual, Jung wrote, "…Man is in need of a symbolic life—badly in need… we have no symbolic life. Where do we live symbolically? Nowhere, except where we participate in the ritual of life." (CW 18 ¶625). Following Jung, Campbell wrote that the purpose of a ritual is "to put oneself in accord with life itself" (Campbell, 1988). In other words, ritual is embodied fantasy—purposeful symbolic action aimed at experiencing the meaning of life itself; in the language of my first dream, discovering the animating breath-soul and honoring it through active participation in its perpetual meaning making function. And much like my initial dream, my training ritual gave me a plan, a goal, and I had in place a wonderful sage dispensing supernatural aid that would help me get to my desired destination. My relationship with Greg grew to become a close personal friendship as well. Not only did he give me my weekly training schedule, but I also received insight and wisdom regarding my body that I was not able to receive through many years of psychoanalysis.

Allow this one example to suffice: Still terrified of open water swimming but with the promises of my initial dream in mind, I vowed to work to overcome my fear of the open water. I swam and swam many laps in the pool. I read several books on swimming. I even attended a four-day workshop by a leading national swim program in Chicago, Illinois. However, I still was not only nervous in the water, I was dreadfully slow. So slow in fact, that I was likely to repeat my experience of being swum over, around, and through if I did not improve. Nonetheless, I persevered. I asked Greg for additional coaching—focusing exclusively on my swim. He agreed and we began meeting on Sunday afternoons at the pool.

Greg watched me, filmed me, and we discussed my swim stroke flaws. After several weeks and noticeable frustration on my part, he said to me from the pool deck, "Hey, you don't look like you are having fun—really. You look like you are just surviving, not really swimming." At that instance, I immediately remembered my first swim experience. I remembered that I had never learned to swim. Even though I had grown up on the shores of Lake Huron, swimming nearly every day possible and with my bedroom less than 20 yards from the shore, I never learned to swim. Even though I had always said how much I loved the water and the deeper the better, I had never taken a swim lesson. Instead, I immediately remembered that I was thrown off the back of a boat at midnight into Lake Huron by my father and had to survive by getting back to the boat. For his part, my father told me that he learned to swim in the same manner and that therefore, I should learn similarly—by crisis. Clearly, that is exactly what I was doing. I was just surviving in the water, hoping to get back to the boat.

Hearing Greg tell me that I was just surviving led me to instantly remember and feel that childhood trauma all over again (CW 16 cf., ¶¶255-293). I then recalled my swim experience in my first triathlon—barely finding my way to shore and clearly exhibiting "survival swimming." Aware of my being lost in myself, Greg asked me if I was alright. We were able to talk about the origin of my swim anxieties, their connection with my awkwardness in the water, and my gratefulness for his insights. In this and many similar ways, Greg served as a new kind of analyst for me. New because I was able to get at complexes and deeply embedded feelings in a way I was not able to otherwise: a new analyst because he offered wisdom and insight regarding the body that I was discovering and its relationship to my breath-soul.

In an effort to become as fast as I could in the water, I would often change my swim workouts to include more sprints and threshold swims in exchange for drills and swim workouts written to specifically address my weaknesses in the water. Noticing my craftiness, Greg asked me why I was changing his swim workouts. When I explained that I felt like I needed to be faster in the water, Greg responded, "I agree completely. However, you won't get fast that way. You only get better by focusing on your weaknesses, especially in the water. If you continue in this manner, you will teach your body to swim bad faster. Stick with what I have written." Sufficiently humbled with this astute wisdom, I thought to myself, "Now that is a metaphor for analytic training!"

After Greg's clear and unambiguous interpretations and my subsequent insights, my swimming became infinitely more enjoyable. I began swimming longer and longer distances and my speeds also began improving. I looked forward to my time in the pool. Unlike biking and running which require much more attention to the road and one's surroundings, long distance swimming invites much more of a deep meditation.

My long swims became a time for me to deeply relax and reflect. Recalling my initial dream, I would breathe purposely and deeply, trying to breathe in from my toes all through my body and then out my nose. In doing so, I was often able to relax to the point where my conscious threshold was lowered and thereby, I could call to mind my most recent dream images and work with them much as Jung had prescribed.

In this way, as I continued to learn to breathe deeply and purposely in the water, my time in the pool became for me a time for meditation and reflection. Also, the fact that

I typically swam early in the morning, often before the sun came up, only further reinforced my sleep-like meditative state. Lastly, I want to stress the point that dreaming with my eyes open was taking place while swimming, honoring my initial dream—that is, it was entirely connected to my body. Perhaps noting my change of attitude in the water, after several months of my new enthusiasm for the water, Greg nicknamed me "the shark."

Chapter 4

One of Many

By this point, my year-long leave of absence from the Jung Institute was nearly ended. As I considered my return to formal analytic training I had very mixed feelings. On the one hand, I still felt very unsure of and questioned my skills and abilities as an analyst-in-training. Also, since two of my training cases dropped out of treatment, I was at the beginning of the Control Stage. I had to decide if I wanted to start over—accruing hours in control supervision as well as analytic hours with my analysands. I was particularly concerned with the financial aspect of training—I would need to continue my personal analysis as well as control supervision for an indefinite period of time. Also, since I was commuting from several hours away, I would continue to have the long hours in the car, the continued cost of the wear and tear on my vehicle, as well as the time away from my family and practice. These were significant concerns, and I felt weighed down with them.

On the other hand, I left on my leave of absence because I was forcing something forward that did not feel honest or genuine. Clearly this was no longer the case. I had a "new analyst" in place and was learning much about myself and my psyche. In fact, much as water promises, I felt like I had been renewed in every sense of the word. Webster's dictionary defines the word renew in the following way, "To make new or as if new again; to make young, fresh, or strong again; to bring back into good condition…To give new spiritual strength to; to make better in spirit; to cause to exist again; to re-establish" (Webster's Dictionary, 1531). In this manner, I felt young and fresh in spirit and certainly felt connected to my Self and my body and knew deep down that this connection was in cooperation with my psyche. I had been given a means through my endurance training to daily connect with my breath-soul and to discover its fantastical workings in my life.

Anxiety and Failure, or Trusting a New Sense of Myself?

As much as I wanted to trust my new-found center, I was still very anxious about my decision. And to be very clear, I also felt selfish about my experiences outside of the Institute during my leave of absence. That is, I was aware of a lingering sense of failure; I imagined that my colleagues must see me as having failed in some essential manner, and that my renewal belonged to me! I was very unsure as well as hesitant about sharing or exposing my experiences to anyone else. I stayed with my tension over many weeks regarding my decision and reflected on it as I swam. Then I had the following dream:

> *I am standing on the shore of a large body of water. I am standing in the water such that I can see deeply into the water with my feet on the bottom. The water was full of life—green*

algae, all different kinds of fish, and an infinite number of different creatures I did not recognize. The Training Director of the Institute was in the middle of the water and was singing a worshipful song to the eggs that were in the water. There were many large white eggs in the water. I remember an incredible feeling of anticipation and patient waiting as well as worship toward these eggs.

When I woke up, I felt as if this dream was a reminder to me of my previous isle people water dream, especially the richness of the water and all that the water promised evidenced in each of the different life forms swimming around me. Moreover, the feeling in the dream was also unmistakably one of belonging, of feeling included amidst the life of the water—I was one of many. Unlike the feelings of being lost, alone, and separate evident during my first dream, in this dream I felt entirely included. To this end, it may be noted that green algae is a photosynthetic organism that is entirely the product of the combination of sun and water, in traditional symbolism, of male and female, and in the language of my first dream, images of Mercurius and anima In this way, the green algae served as a loving reminder of having worked to incorporate my breath soul under the watchful presence of a life-giving warmth. And the fact that my feet were clearly planted on the floor of the water indicated to me that my position was grounded, was solid, and moreover afforded me a panoramic view of all of the water life around me.

From this comprehensive viewpoint, I saw the Director of Training out in the middle of the water singing a worship song to white eggs. Certainly, I was aware of the symbolism of eggs, especially their relationship to Easter, and thereby, to a process of death, transformation, and re-birth prefigured in my first dream. And the fact that the eggs were white seemed to indicate a pureness; the color white also figuring into the traditions of many cultures during rituals of initiation (cf., *Herder Symbol Dictionary*, 214).

The anticipatory feelings surrounding the white eggs including the worshipful song sung to them by the Director of Training indicated to me that there was much more to come. To realize this promise, she exhibited "a patient waiting." In considering my essentially having to start my control stage over again, such a patient waiting seemed entirely appropriate to the situation were I to re-engage. Again, it should be clearly stated, that this dream, as with the first, seemed to underscore process (patient waiting, watching the water life, noticing the algae) as opposed to product/outcome.

After considering the dream and its images carefully, I decided to re-engage with the Institute and pursue finishing my analytic training. In so doing, I promised myself that I would attempt to keep these dream images in front of me at all times, as reminders of what I had been initiated into—especially all the different life forms around me and remind myself that I am included. As much as I felt like a pariah upon leaving the Institute and thus, feeling no sense of acceptance whatsoever, I now began to feel like a pilgrim. My numinous experiences were incorruptible. As Campbell (1949) intimated, my pilgrimage now was to return to the Institute and share the numinous I had experienced, and in this way, renew those similarly engaged in their pilgrimages. In the language of my second dream, to join in the worship-filled song of life and its promise of renewal knowing that wherever my journeys took me, my feet were solidly planted.

To this end, I signed up for two ½ Ironman events for the following year in addition to many running events. I had not completed any long-distance triathlons and thus, was completely overwhelmed by any thought of the distances. I would need to swim nearly one and one-half miles in open water, then bike 56 miles, and finish with a half-marathon (13.1 miles). I placed all my trust in Greg and together we developed a training plan that would get me to the finish line. I trained very hard, looking forward each week to receiving my new training plan. I would read, then re-read, and continue to re-read it throughout the week, draining every ounce of meaning from it.

My first ½ Ironman took place in Muncie, Indiana in July. I struggled through the swim, was "off course" several times but finished. The bike was made much more difficult by the heat and humidity which then really took its toll during the run portion. Nonetheless, I finished in a very respectable 5 hours and 50 minutes, placing 463rd out of 791 total men and 46th out of 91 men within my age group. Two weeks later, I completed my second triathlon at this distance bettering my time (5:41) and felt very pleased with my year. At the finish line of both events, Greg was there to meet and congratulate me. Having placed so much trust in him, and aware of his link with all my dream work, his presence gave me such a feeling of fulfillment and purpose—I was very grateful for his leadership helping me to realize my accomplishments and having been given the strength, both physical and psychic to make it to the finish lines.

The following year, I also completed several ½ Ironman triathlons again bettering my time (5:27) and feeling stronger and stronger, both physically and spiritually. In addition, during this period of time, I had several new referrals for patients seeking analysis such that I was able to begin to accumulate hours for my control work. My practice continued to grow and grow and again, I felt very blessed.

In this manner, my days began taking consistent form. I would receive my training plan on Sunday and then see my week of training. Usually, I would wake up very early each morning and train, beginning the day spending time and energy connecting to my breath-soul, engaging in my deep meditation, and exercising with my soul. To this end, it is written in Proverbs: "Honour thy Lord with thy substance, and with the first fruits of all thine increase: So shall thy barns be filled with plenty, and thy presses shall burst out with new wine (Proverbs 3:9, King James Version).

I rearranged my practice hours such that I began my professional day by mid-morning and worked until early evening. My training usually left me feeling invigorated and full of energy, energy that I then spent during my day, knowing deep down that I was in accordance with my own breath-soul. My body underwent many physical changes. Since my leave of absence from analytic training, I had lost 75 lbs., 14 inches from my waist, and my body fat measured at 7%. Many patients and professional colleagues noticed my enthusiasm and weight loss and would comment—some fearing that I was ill, others curious what I was up to. I proudly explained that I had been introduced to endurance sports and was training for long distance triathlons and road running events.

The year (2005) ended with a very notable experience. I spent the second half of the year training for the Columbus Marathon, my second attempt at the full marathon distance. My stated goal in running Columbus was to qualify for the Boston Marathon in my age group. To do so, I would need to run 3:20:59 or less. My training had gone very well, and my races leading up to Columbus had given Greg and me every reason to believe that Boston was within my reach. I arrived in Columbus and my anxieties began setting in—so much so in fact, that I began doubting myself and my goal.

At the pre-race expo, I signed up to participate in the pacer program in an effort to quiet my anxieties. This would allow me to follow a "pacer," an experienced marathoner who was to run specific mile splits, and thus arrive at the finish line within my desired goal time. On race morning, the pacer did not show up until just seconds before the gun went off—not a good sign. In addition to running even splits, the pacer is also charged with the responsibility of motivating the runners within his/her group. My pacer was not a pleasant person and within the first five miles, had repeatedly run miles that were as much as 30 and 45 seconds faster than goal pace. In a race of this distance (26.2 miles), this level of variance over the first miles can be very detrimental.

And so, after seven miles, I made a decision to trust my own training, something I should have done in the first place. I was able to settle into a rhythm and began running miles at my goal pace. At the marathon's half-way mark, I planned to meet my wife who was to hand me my nutrition for the second half of the marathon.

Columbus is known for its large number of spectators who line the streets and cheer for the runners. Although my wife and I had done our due diligence the day before and scoped out a specific spot to meet—on race day, no spots are reserved, and she was not there. Moreover, when I did hear her call my name while running after me, I was too far ahead of her to retreat. I reasoned, "No problem, I will go to plan B." Because of the layout of the course, my wife would meet me in three more miles on the opposite side of the block. I thought I would just need to hang on until then.

So, I settled in and after three miles, began looking for my wife. I spotted her up ahead and thought I would have plenty of room for her to pass me my nutrition. I angled over to her side of the road and readied myself to grab my calories. However, when I caught up to her, she held her hands out and they were empty! Empty! What? I did not have a plan C. I was at a complete loss! I thought to myself, "OK, not the best of situations; just make the most of things and see what happens." By that point, I had learned that in endurance sports, all energy counts and if one is using it by getting upset, that energy is not available later when it is really needed. After the marathon, I learned that my nutrition had apparently fallen out of my wife's pocket when she was trying to run to catch up with me and therefore, she had nothing to give me.

Running down the road in Columbus, I recalled my isle people water dream and was again, filled with a warm feeling. On the outside, I was tired, hungry, and very sore. My lungs hurt and burned from running too hard in the first half of the marathon. However, deep down inside, I had energy and a place to live as I finished the marathon. I decided to just do the best I could and accept whatever would happen. On that day, that would be all I could do to honor my dreams.

The further I ran, the more I struggled. That is, I was on pace to qualify until mile 18 and then my lack of calories made itself known. I did come upon an aid station that had energy gels which I took in although my body was already too far gone and to finish, I would have to really push myself very hard. I ran as hard and as consistently as I could and focused on the fact that my wife and kids would be at the finish line to see me home.

I did finish the Columbus marathon. I ran it in 3:32, 12 minutes over my qualifying time but bettering my time from Detroit by over 75 minutes! I was very disappointed in one sense, but in another I was proud that I was able to make the most of the situation. I was disappointed that I did not trust my inner confidence and training as I had in other events—that I let my anxiety get the upper hand. However, as I was thinking over my race wrapped in my marathon mylar blanket and hobbling around the finisher's area, a young runner sought me out and came over and, unannounced, gave me a big hug. He said, "Hey, you don't know how much you helped me out there! I was dying out there and you were a rock. You don't know this, but I have been following you for the last 10 miles. This is my first marathon, and I could not have finished without you—you were so consistent and strong. Thanks!" I really did not know what to say. His words caught me much like the conversation with the woman on Belle Isle, and all I could offer in return was to genuinely accept his thanks and wish him well in his marathon recovery.

In considering my experiences in Columbus, it might be imagined as an experience of the trickster archetype. Specifically, rather than follow my own inner guide, my own breath-soul, I fell victim to my anxieties—my worries and my feelings of not being capable. Such an attitude is contrary to my isle people water dream when I say, "I can do that." By identifying with my anxieties, I was not fed, I did not have the psychic calories to meet my goal. In this way, I was tricked and only later was made aware that the day was to be very different than I had imagined it. I left Columbus thinking to myself, "Clearly, the lesson for today is: Sometimes you win because you meet your goals, and sometimes you win because others are able to meet their goals through you—this was not my day but it was his. OK, I can celebrate that!"

In addition, I was again made aware of the incredible spiritual nature of these endurance events. Each of the athletes seeking to discover that special sense of purpose and meaning—whether that is a specific finishing time goal, just finishing itself, or finding a guiding spirit within that one was previously unaware of. In addition, I was also made aware of how I was being used to aid someone else in meeting their marathon goal. In this way, I was reminded of Jung's comment in his autobiography regarding his dream of the yogi—in other words, who is dreaming whom? I left Columbus with a sense of awe, complete awe, perhaps much more so than if I were to have qualified for the Boston marathon.

My clinical practice continued to grow as did my clinical confidence. And as Greg and I reviewed my year, we decided that I would be able to step up to the next level of triathlon competition: The Ironman. As I stated, this event consisted of a 2 ½ mile open water swim, a 112-mile bike ride, and then a full marathon. Due to there being only 21 Ironman events in the world at that time, and only six in the United States, deciding on which event was critical. We considered my professional obligations, my analytic training requirements, my family commitments, and finally, my physical skills, as well as when each event occurred during the calendar year. We settled on Ironman Wisconsin, in Madison.

Chapter 5

Dream Trophy

For Ironman Wisconsin, I completed 468 hours of training over 24 weeks that included 180 miles of swimming, 4000 miles of bicycling, and finally, 1053 miles of running. The numbers of training hours and miles do not tell the real story of Ironman, however. Instead I want to focus on several key events and experiences I had while training that proved pivotal during my Ironman race and link those with my previous insights and understandings.

To say I was nervous when I signed up for Ironman would be a gross understatement. I was terrified. Ironman events sell out within only a few hours of going on sale—and they go on sale the morning following the specific event. Roughly 2000 entries sold within a matter of minutes. Therefore, I decided to drive to Madison and stay several nights so that I could first witness the Ironman as a spectator and then be in line the next morning. I was so excited about being in the company of these athletes and the Ironman community that I could not sleep the night before. I was not nervous or anxious, I was simply so full of enthusiasm and excitement that I could not rest. Rather than resist it, I got up and drove downtown to the Ironman Village, the site of the start/finish line. I walked the streets in excitement and when the workers began setting up the finish shoot, I began eliciting from them their "Ironman stories."

Soon enough the event was underway, and it was a day of extremes with 95-degree temperatures and blustery winds with a record number of DNFs (did not finish). I blocked out that fact and again, after difficulty sleeping, was in line very early the next morning with the other Ironman hopefuls. I paid the fee, made hotel arrangements, and with that I was in the car and on my way home signed up for my first Ironman.

Ironman Training

Thus, began my training for my first Ironman. On the one hand, I was securely re-engaged at the Institute, navigating through the Control Stage, writing and participating in colloquia (the formal presentation of one's professional work to the Institute community), and continuing my analysis and control work. On the other hand, I was equally secure in my relationship with my coach, my body analysis, and continued to be informed by my numinous experiences in my long-distance endurance training and events. However, training for Ironman would require even more submission to the energies within. That is, the training, between 15 and 25 hours per week for 24 plus weeks at a time, is such that it can only be accomplished by connecting to something within that is not only physical but, in fact compliments the physical. As Joseph Campbell stated, "Sacrifice equals bliss. You die to your flesh and are thus, born to your spirit. You learn that your body is simply the carrier of your spirit" (Campbell, 1988).

Or to put it differently, one of my teammates wrote,

Chapter 5: Dream Trophy

> Ironman is a funny way to celebrate life. No one can tell you about it, you must discover it for yourself. It calls for an extreme sense of dedication and perseverance with a dashing flare of humor. Always the spectators, family, friends, and volunteers are the heroes of the day. The whole event is made up of free souls escaping from the ordinary social conventions and rising above mediocrity. What you gain from training and toeing the line is good and is never truly lost. It stays a part of a person, becomes part of their character. Do not try and analyze it, just have faith that everything changes color when you experience your own little miracles of the day. (James, 2006).

This quote was written by a fellow triathlon team member after she completed Ironman Wisconsin in a race report to our triathlon team. It is an Ironman custom to write a race report, to give back to the team something of your personal experiences of the day, a very treasured amulet team members can then use to remind themselves of the energies present within. In her report, the recognition and respect for the level of commitment necessary to complete an Ironman is implicit, its extra-ordinariness evident, and thus, its relationship to the Divine, is laid bare. Also implicit is the dangerous impossibility of the Ironman competition itself, hence the hopeful experience of "miracles" needed along the journey in order to successfully find one's way to the finish line. And finally, a loving plea to let go, to "have faith" and know that miracles do happen when you are able to see the colors change.

My Ironman training became a very treasured ritual. It is very hard to describe. The hours and miles are absurd as is the discipline to train for such an event. I wish to highlight only a few key elements of my training. First, the word discipline deserves attention. Webster's dictionary defines discipline thus: "instruction, training, a learner" (*Webster's Dictionary*, 520). This definition is very apt. I completely submitted my life and schedule to my training, and thus was receiving instruction for a new type of education. I relied heavily on many of my teammates who had completed Ironman triathlons. I took in their thoughts, advice, and knowledge. In so doing, I was being initiated into a new level of relationship with them—If I listened carefully, and if things went my way on race day, I would be an Ironman.

The only guarantees available were that the training would be very tough, the road usually difficult, and that I should be prepared for many things to "go wrong." That is, I was to trust my training (my discipline) no matter what occurred; that things will go wrong but that is also part of the training process; and finally, I was to learn the true meaning of the mantra, "Keep moving forward." This phrase is an Ironman tradition. I learned: it does not mean go forward at all costs—to do so would be foolish, would likely lead to injury, or at a minimum would certainly lead to burnout. Instead, the phrase came to mean: each day find and learn to listen to the quiet voice within; learn to trust that voice no matter what others say or life brings you; and finally, trust that when you are listening, you are doing what you are supposed to be doing. Again, this advice was entirely consistent with my two previous dreams and further reinforced the spiritual nature of my training ritual. It is quite common to hear a fellow triathlete say, "Keep moving forward" during trying periods of training or competition in which another athlete is struggling and needs to reconnect to the deep energies within.

Second, I want to highlight the role of fantasy and prayer. Most of my weekend training consisted of early morning swims, followed by bicycle rides of four hours or longer, immediately followed by runs of 30 to 60 minutes. During

Chapter 5: Dream Trophy

the long training hours, I listened to music or prayed. As I did so and much like my swimming, I found that often my thoughts would coalesce around certain themes. One theme that I continually mused on was what I came to call "The cycle of the corn." It just struck me as so meaningful: As I ran the country roads of rural Northwestern Indiana during the winter months, the farmlands were so desolate, one might even say abandoned. The wind would snap and bite me as it whipped off the fields since there were no crops to shelter me.

As spring found its way home, the fields would begin to open up, the ground softened and moistened by spring rains, and I envisaged the change much like a woman in those last few moments before childbirth—her body instinctively opening wide to reveal life. Within a few weeks, the crops would begin to grow, and I could measure the amount of sunshine and rain we were having by the size of the crops that day. As the season drew on, the crops were often so tall as to completely envelope me as I rode my bike or ran along. Then, just as the crop had reached its peak and was to become food, the late summer and early fall became race season—time to toe the line and pray for small miracles. That is, having been nurtured by a season of training, of communion with my breath-soul, of time with teammates, it was now time to give it all back in the form of competition—to die to ourselves and ideally, find a safe, secure mount to escape the bounds of mediocrity.

I often prayed that I could be more like the corn—to serve one's inherent purpose in life to the fullest, knowingly and lovingly dependent on all the variables surrounding me for my sustenance, and then to die with the grace and dignity of giving back by way of feeding others such that life itself moves forward.

The final theme that was a constant during my Ironman training was prayer. Everything just seemed like such a mix of absolute and utter impossibility with beautiful, spirit-filled moments of insight—with very little in between. Yes, the training plans were read as holy writ, and yes, I was well aware of the meaningfulness of my experiences all along the way—but this was not enough on most days. The daunting awareness of the physical challenges necessary each day, let alone each week was overwhelming. I found that if I just began praying, I could bring myself a great deal of peace. Moreover, I typically found myself praying an old Gnostic prayer that I had learned when I first began contemplating entering analytic training. The prayer is as follows:

> *According to what Thou, Greatest One saidest unto me, would that a Voice might come daily, to awaken me; such that I may not stumble and fall prey to the powers of this world.*

This prayer has always felt very comforting and meaningful. In hindsight, it seems to capture many of the themes from my two dreams, especially the prayerful request to be reminded to seek the Divine in all one does, to be awakened, and re-awakened, as William Blake said, "To see Eternity in an hour." In addition, implicit in the prayer is also the need to be mindful of the ways in which the powers of the world impede my being able to do this—for me getting caught in my anxieties and worries and stumbling. Finally, the dream also implies a ready connection to hearing/sensing the Divine, in this instance, via the transcendent function and thereby reawakening to the voice within. In the language of Ironman, "Keep moving forward."

And so it was. With discipline, prayer, and participation in what I felt to be a sacred ritual, I completed the training and was preparing to leave for Madison, Wisconsin. I checked my bike, readied my wet suit, and ensured all my race clothes were wear-tested and ready to go. Several nights prior to leaving for Wisconsin I had the following dream:

> *I was in a large room and part of an awards ceremony. I was working behind the scenes and helping to make things go smoothly. Then suddenly, my name was called. I remember sweeping the floors and helping set up chairs and then my name was called. I was handed a large trophy that was Eros—depicted as a winged footed athlete. The trophy said, 'The Words of Ironman' and had various philosophical phrases engraved on it. I started crying when I received the trophy."*

This dream continues to carry a tremendous amount of very positive feeling for me. When I had the dream, I was completely immersed in my training and all that it meant to me. I felt as if I had been truly blessed—I had been able to find something in my life that continued to feed me spiritually, and I was far from satiation. I had established a great circle of friends, my clinical practice was doing well, and I was continuing to progress through the Institute. Perhaps this is imaged in the dream as my "workman" status—participating behind the scenes to help make things go smoothly.

Jung has variously defined the term Eros as a harmonizing energy regulating the relations between spirit and instinct (CW 7 ¶¶16-34), as the principle of relatedness within the psyche (cf., CW 10 ¶¶236-275) and also as a "kosmogonos," a "creator father-mother of all higher consciousness" (Jung, 1965). Guggenbühl-Craig (1980) described Eros as a psychological characteristic that makes Gods and humans loving, creative, and involved. And Hillman (1985) opines that whereas *anima* attracts one's attention so as to illumine, Eros turns pure reflection (illumination) into relationship, into an active process of soul-making.

It is equally vital to note the specific relationship between Aphrodite and Eros. That is, much as Aphrodite was said to have been born out of the water and is therefore related to the renewal energies of water (cf., Edinger, 1985, 54), so her son may be equally linked to transformation—specific periods where human limitedness makes itself known. This is also an example of what Jung meant when he stated that Eros is a god that is invoked when we transcend our human limits (Jung, 1965)

It seems quite fitting then, that the Eros trophy was being awarded at this Ironman ceremony. And with many of my illuminations being associated with water (e.g. Belle Isle, the water people, the female water companion, the water full of life, as well my swimming challenges), it also seemed fitting that Aphrodite's son would be honored on the trophy. The fact that I was given the trophy is still too much to grasp—I can still only cry and know that I have been touched by something that far encompasses anything I could have wished for. To have had this dream when I did is an experience of Divinity that lets me know I am held and contained.

The days leading up to an Ironman are filled with nervous energy. In large part the energy is a product of the Ironman taper. That is, after training for 20 plus hours a week for as many as 24 weeks, the Ironman athlete then gradually tapers over a period of just a couple of weeks to the point of training as few as 5 to 7 hours in the week leading up to the event. Rather than feeling like a comfort or even a long sought-after rest, such a taper exposes the incredible mix of neurochemistry and musculature necessary to fuel the body to complete the Ironman triathlon. In short, it is a feeling of boundless energy racing through one's body and mind coupled with

Chapter 5: Dream Trophy

the injunction to stay off your feet and do as little as possible throughout the day. What a clash of opposites!

Nonetheless, I checked off every item from my list, packed up my vehicle, and along with my wife and family, made my way to Wisconsin. Again, I found my way into the Ironman community, except this time as a competitor. The set-up and preparation for an event of this magnitude is impressive. The athlete has to be checked in to the event which includes many long lines, picking up your race numbers and course information as well as being formally weighed in case of medical emergency during the event.

In addition to the usual transition area (the area designated for one's bike assignment), Ironman triathlon also allows each athlete two "special needs bags" (portable transition areas) one each to be delivered to the athlete at the half-way points on the bicycle and run courses. These bags are special for many reasons. In addition to ensuring one's preferred calories and necessary supplies (e.g. extra bicycle tire inner tubes, or a dry shirt), it also allows for special messages of encouragement from one's family and supporters. Once packed, these bags are sealed and then dropped off at designated points in the city in order for the Ironman race officials to pack them properly for delivery on race day.

Over the next two days, I completed all the required paperwork; delivered all my race materials to their proper places; checked (and rechecked) my gear several times. Everything was done. Despite all of the excitement and nervous energy in the air, I was aware of an impenetrable quiet and calm within me that I could access again and again as necessary. This feeling was appreciably different from my feelings prior to the Columbus marathon, as an example. I was ready and I knew it. All that was left was to offer my prayers of thanksgiving. To do so, I made a specific point to check the local downtown community for a Catholic church during my short training runs leading up to the event. I found a church only several blocks from our hotel. My family and I attended evening mass and afterward I had my dinner and found my way to bed.

The weather forecast was not good. Generally, forecasters were calling for temperatures far below the September average with strong, gusting winds and intermittent rain. In fact, by race morning, the forecast had worsened such that the rain would be a constant and the temperatures were not expected to rise above the mid to upper forties.

Curiously, I slept reasonably well. In the past, this had always been a measure of my feeling deep down my preparedness for the event at hand—and so it was. That is, despite being only a matter of minutes from my event, I still felt entirely connected to my quiet calm within. After eating my breakfast, I gathered my equipment and headed to my transition area. I double checked my bicycle, all my nutrition, and then put on my wetsuit for the swim leg. By this point, the rain was a constant, the winds were increasing, and the air temperature felt "cold." Before leaving my transition area I said a quiet prayer: I promised myself that no matter what the day would bring, I would seek to draw on my quiet calm; I would be fed by my numinous experiences leading me to this point; I would trust my training and early morning prayerful meditations; and finally, I would also trust my coach and his wisdom. To be very clear, I was aware of the nervous energy in the air, but I was not going to fall into it. With that, I ended my prayer and joined the walk of athletes as we made our way to the water's edge.

With as cold as the air felt, the water felt warm as I entered—thankfully. I waded out and worked to just stay focused on my task. Later I was to learn that this would be a record open water swim start for Ironman; over 2500 athletes

Chapter 5: Dream Trophy

would begin their Ironman Triathlon journey that morning in the waters of Lake Monona. Again, the National Anthem was sung, the gun went off, and with that the churn and swell of an Ironman swim start was now underway.

I was kicked, banged, and wrestled throughout the first several hundred yards. Focusing on my inner calm and confidence, I smiled through the splashes and worked to just focus on sighting the buoys and monitoring my body and its signals. Sighting was made especially difficult due to the wind and consequent swells, but with that number of athletes in the water, it is more a matter of following and trusting one another as much as relying exclusively on one's own sighting. Before I knew it, we had rounded the fourth turn buoy and had begun lap number two. A very quick look at my watch told me I had met my time target and with that I set off to the first turn buoy again. The second lap was more difficult—on the second lap, I chose to swim closer to the turn buoys, but this meant that I would have to contend with many of the stronger swimmers (the shortest distance between two points is a straight line). I did all right, looking up during breaths and thinking often of my "water dreams" and hoping that someone somewhere was taking all this in and laughing!

Shortly thereafter I was out of the water, up the parking helix and into the hotel where one of the conference rooms had been turned into a makeshift dressing room. Later I was to learn that a record number of athletes (39) failed to finish the swim, many just choosing to swim to shore and thus, dropping out of the event all together. A volunteer helped me out of my wet suit and assisted me getting dressed into my biking clothes. A double check to ensure I had my nutrition on board, and I was out the door to pick up my bike from the transition area. My wife and kids were waiting next to the fence aligning the area. Despite the rain and wind, they were all smiles and yelled encouragement. Several kisses blown in their direction and I was off on my bicycle odyssey.

The 112-mile bicycle ride would prove very, very difficult. The rain worsened as did the winds to the point that it was often very difficult to even see the road. In fact, the wind gusted so fiercely that many athletes were walking their bikes down Madison's rolling hills—something I have never witnessed in a triathlon prior or after. That is, many, many, many times the wind blew so hard as to either force the athlete off the road entirely, and/or rattle/shake the bicycle's wheels several inches in both directions. In short, the traction was treacherous. By the end of the ride, my arms throbbed and ached from simply holding my handlebars so tightly. Although I did not crash, I unfortunately was witness to many horrendous bicycle accidents—one in particular occurred right beside me as we crossed over a set of wet and slippery railroad tracks. The accident was so serious that I helped to call for an ambulance before resuming my ride.

At several points throughout the bike ride, my mettle was tested and then retested. I knew the bicycle course well. Several months prior to the event, my family and I made our way to Madison and I rode the course several times. On this day, however, the bicycle course did not resemble the course I rode. After a particularly difficult climb up one of Madison's hills, I saw this guy screaming at me through the rain and from beneath a hooded sweatshirt pulled up over his head. It was Greg! I did not expect to see him, he had never told me he would be present, and his presence completely changed my energy and served as a loving reminder of what I had accomplished to get to this point, and what I would need to do to finish on this day. He asked about my body. What was I feeling? What about my nutrition? And with a dashing flare of humor, told me that "I looked great." That was funny!

With that, I finished the 112 bicycle miles and felt every last ounce of the difficulties of the ride. I had trouble dismounting my bike, but as is the Ironman custom, there was a volunteer right at my side, helping me to balance. I hobbled back into the same hotel conference room to change as another volunteer then took my bicycle back to my transition area. However, when I got into the conference room, what I saw really scared me! The room was full of other athletes, many sitting down vomiting, and others huddled into small groups so as to increase their warmth. This scene did not allow me to deny how difficult the day was—I was looking at it. I grabbed my bag of run clothes, found an open seat, and soon a volunteer made his way to my side. I looked at him and saw that he had an "Ironman Finisher" t-shirt on and thereby felt very comforted. He saw that I was rattled by the scene, and he said to me, "Don't pay any attention to that—you look strong—stop looking around—just let me help you get dressed and you will finish this thing." His help was crucial since my fingers were not working yet due to the cold, and my arms continued to throb. Soon enough and with his assistance, I was dressed and headed out on the marathon course. At the first turn I saw my wife and kids and stopped to give them each a kiss. With their well wishes in hand and 114.4 miles down, I was out to complete the last 26.2 miles.

With the bicycle miles still very fresh in my mind, and the recent images of the dressing room pressing in on me, I felt spooked to say the least. I looked at my watch to notice that my heart rate was 140 beats per minute. That was my ideal training zone that I used all summer long as a gauge for my training intensity. It is hard to over-estimate how much comfort that number brought me that afternoon through the rain and wind. That is, I was spooked, and was beginning to fall into an abyss of anxiety, but deep down my body knew exactly what to do and was right on target, precisely as I had trained. After that, I found my smile again and resumed my thoughts of my dreams, my training experiences, and the fact that I was actually competing in an Ironman!

Within the first four or five marathon miles, I again found this hooded guy running next me! Greg began asking, "How are you doing?" "Tell me about your body!" "Where are you at with your nutrition?" "What did you think about that bike ride?" I smiled, answered him, and explained that I was aware this was a very difficult day. He relayed that everyone's times, including the professionals, were all far behind due to the weather—that I was right on target for my training, that my body knew what to do, and to just stay smart with my pace and nutrition. With that, he was gone again, and I was left alone with my thoughts and reflections. It is important to again point out that an Ironman course encompasses 140.6 miles; Greg was able to navigate the distance despite the weather conditions and two thousand other athletes to share his coaching wisdom and words of encouragement with me multiple times which meant everything on this difficult day.

The rain, the wind, and the cold began to usher in the night. Miles and miles went by, and the darkness of the night settled in. As I turned down a dark street, I heard my name being called. I struggled through the darkness and rain to understand what was happening. As I approached, I could see it was Greg, this time with an amplified megaphone and he was sharing with the crowd my accomplishment saying, "Ladies and gentleman, this is Warren Sibilla from South Bend, IN, in another 13.1 miles he will be an Ironman—Keep going Warren, you are looking great!" Again, I was picked up out of my marathon daze and reminded of my goal, why I was there, and that I had loving company no matter how dark the night or difficult the journey. Keep moving forward.

Chapter 5: Dream Trophy

With that I entered the special needs area to re-equip myself for the last half of the marathon. I changed my socks and shoes, gathered up my nutrition, and changed into a dry shirt and jacket. Finally, at the bottom of my bag, I found framed pictures of my wife and kids that had pre-recorded audio messages playing, "You can do it daddy; we love you! You are almost there! You are very strong. We will be at the finish line waiting for you!" Again, love around every corner! Little did I know I was being filmed on national television as I again wiped tears from my eyes.

With dry clothes and pockets filled with energy, I began the second half of the marathon. I saw my wife and kids on the side of the road. I thought to myself, "Here were the real heroes!" They had to endure the extremes of the weather while waiting for long, extended periods of time only to be rewarded with a brief glimpse as I slipped by. More kisses and a promise, "Stay up with me—don't go to sleep, I am almost done and soon, very soon, we are going to celebrate!"

The second half of the marathon proved difficult. The streets were very dark, the wind howled, and the rain never lessened. Still, I managed to match the time from my first half. By now most of my athlete colleagues still engaged in the triathlon were walking and/or only managing what is often termed the "death march." The day, the weather, the event, the miles, all had taken their toll. To finish now, I would need to draw on something other than physical energy.

I also began to walk for short periods to give my legs a rest. As I did so, I recalled walking the streets of Detroit during the last mile of my first marathon. "What happened between then and now" I asked myself? With ease, I could feel the same warm feelings within, I celebrated all that had been experienced, and was carried along by my sense of communion with the energies within. I began thanking all the volunteers I could spot along the route. One last connection with Greg who had again managed to find me on the marathon route, and I knew I was almost home.

As is the Ironman custom, if the athlete chooses, his/her family can run the finisher's shoot with the athlete. The athlete running next to me asked if my family was waiting for me. When I answered in the affirmative, he said, "You are much stronger than I am right now, go ahead and finish ahead of me, I'm going to rest a moment and then I will go behind you." With that, I turned the corner to find my wife and children waiting for me in the middle of the shoot. Arm in arm with my family, I finished the Wisconsin Ironman triathlon in 13 hours, 36 minutes, and 31 seconds. I was an Ironman finisher.

To preserve my Ironman experience, I purchased a DVD with my finish as well as highlights from the day. However, when my DVD arrived and I watched it, only the highlights of the day were recorded. When it came time for my finish, the recording went black. As I talked with the recording company, I learned that due to the extremes of weather their camera malfunctioned—they did not have a recording of my finish. I thought, "OK, I have my experiences deep inside myself." However, when watching the national broadcast of Ironman Wisconsin on television, I saw that I was on their film at several points throughout the course, the final one being my whole family's finish! What an end to an amazing experience and again, love and containment around every corner.

Perhaps then the Eros trophy might be understood thus: The trophy represents an ability to navigate the psychic waters between spirit and body; to take in the illuminations and reflections of psyche and make them tangible; and in so doing, experience the creative function of the psyche, namely finding a loving, secure mount on an escaping soul leaving the bounds of mediocrity. To quote Jung (1965),

> The decisive question for man is: Is he related to something infinite or not… Unconscious wholeness therefore seems to me the true spiritus rector of all biological and psychic events. Here is a principle that strives for total realization—which in man's case signifies the attainment of total consciousness…and self-knowledge is the heart and essence of this process. (324-5)

Chapter 6

Spiritus Rector

I remained high from my Ironman experience for many months following the triathlon. Having put in the time, effort and discipline to train for Ironman, I felt as if I could try and complete one additional event before the end of the year. I settled on the Chicago Lake front Ultra-Marathon, a 50-kilometer road race event (approximately 31 miles). Greg and I wrote a plan that would get me to the finish line, but I would need to be especially sensitive to any signs of over-training or injury. I managed the training very well with my primary energy coming from my meditations on my Ironman experiences—a rich well of energy that felt limitless.

I had this dream the night before the ultra-marathon:

> *I was in a park and was watching a couple play with a dog. They were tossing a Frisbee back and forth and the dog was catching it and bringing it back. Everyone was smiling and the feeling was one of just pure play and joy.*

I awoke and with a look out the window I was not sure what the dream had to do with my day. It really made no sense to me! It was dark with gusting, howling winds (greater than 30 mph), and pouring rain. This combined with the thirty-degree temperatures promised another very difficult day! And the fact that the race would take place along the lake front only underscored the likely challenges of the day. With just several hundred participants, the ultra-marathon was completely different from Ironman. Not only were there very, very few volunteers, the few aid stations that were available were self-serve. Indeed, a few jugs of water and some paper cups—most of which had blown away. Wow! This would be a very different experience.

Nonetheless, the National Anthem was played, and we were off. The race was set up to include three out and back loops (approx. 20K, 15K and 15K) to ensure a watchful presence on all competitors. The wind was sharply out of the North, which meant that on the "out laps" I struggled, at times feeling like I was simply standing still with my legs moving. However, on the "in laps" I felt like I could recover and re-gather my strength.

I did well on the first two laps, running at a pace consistent with my training. I was able to gather strength from my family, who were at the start/finish line, as I ended and began each loop. My meditations during the day often focused on the water, Lake Michigan, thinking about all of my water dreams and how I had worked with them. However, when beginning the third loop, I said to my wife, "This is really getting hard!" I was beginning the last nine miles, the miles that would take me further than I had ever run, and I was feeling my season; I was tired. I loaded up my pockets with my calories and headed out.

I struggled through the first four miles or so—telling myself that I just needed to get to the turnaround point. Once there, I would have the "wind on my side" and the "wind would carry me home safely." I arrived at the turn around, headed home and as I did so, I ran through the same park I had encountered five times earlier during the day. This time, however, I noticed a young couple playing Frisbee with a dog. What? Rain, howling wind, and freezing temperatures—this just did not make sense. I looked closer figuring I was dangerously low on calories and hallucinating. Yes, indeed, a couple playing Frisbee with a dog in the park—this was the exact image from my dream! I instantly began laughing out loud. I thought, "That is it. It is all about playing. Playing! However absurd—Play! That is what Jung meant—Don't be afraid to play! Play was a very apt synonym for the transcendent function. When one can play, truly play, there is another reality." Again, I was filled with the now very familiar warm feelings I had felt in previous events. I thought of my winged Eros trophy dream and imagined the wind was indeed moving me toward the finish line—my trophy already in hand. I thought this was what Jung meant by living with the unconscious as a "co-determining factor," by playing, and thereby changing the "centre of psychic gravity," and this experience producing some-thing that is incorruptible—a diamond body (CW 13 ¶67). Living in this manner, with this type of psychic awareness, is to continually honor the *spiritus rector* of life itself.

After receiving my finisher's medal, I learned that I had, in fact, finished fourth in my age group—quite an accomplishment for my first ultra-marathon. I drove home feeling exhausted, aching and sore, but also quite aware that this had been an incredible year, with so many insights, and I could not wait to dive into next year.

My play dream is so simplistic and joyous that in one sense, no interpretation seems necessary, at least in hindsight. Nonetheless, in light of the previous three dreams, one can certainly note the interplay between masculine and feminine with the circular disc perhaps an indication of the Self, the medium being one of play/fantasy. The fact that the dream occurred at the end of my season and just prior to preparation of my thesis is especially noteworthy; the dream serving as a loving reminder to not get caught in a mess of anxieties, but rather seek to play, to be open to play, and to seek to play with others.

To this end, it seems apt to offer a lengthy summary of the psychological need to play by Donald Winnicott (1971):

> The searching can come only from desultory formless functioning, or perhaps from rudimentary playing, as if in a neutral zone. It is only here, in this unintegrated state of the personality, that which we describe as creative can appear. This if reflected back, but only if reflected back, becomes part of the personality, and eventually this in summation makes the individual to be, to be found; and eventually enables himself or herself to postulate the existence of the self. This gives us our indication for therapeutic procedure—to afford opportunity for formless experience, and for creative impulses, motor and sensory, which are the stuff of playing. And on the basis of playing is built the whole of man's experiential existence. No longer are we either introvert or extrovert. We experience life in the area of transitional phenomena, in the exciting interweave of subjectivity and objective observation, and in an area that is intermediate between the inner reality of the individual and the shared reality of the world that is external to individuals (64).

What a beautiful dream and a very fitting description that both serve to frame my previous experiences nicely. What Winnicott has called "desultory formless functioning," in the "unintegrated state personality" is known in Jungian literature as *teleos*, synchronicity, and facilitated by the transcendent function. Winnicott highlighted the need to have this play reflected back, to have it received into consciousness and that as a consequence, one's creativity is fostered. Through the birthing of this creativity, one is then able to see the workings of a self.

In the language of my dreams, this would be demonstrated by my respecting the isle people and their message to breathe deeply and purposely, to trust my *anima*-breath-soul, and thereby, share in the sacred ritual of life itself. When I have trusted my *anima*-breath-soul, synchronicities appeared, doors opened, and love was found around every corner; I was afforded a view of the rich water life; and I was awarded a trophy of Eros. I am pleased that Winnicott highlighted the therapy (read therapeutics, soul-healing) inherent in the formless play of motor and sensory, that I have found through long-distance endurance sports. And while Winnicott struggles to name precisely the "exciting interweave between inner and outer worlds," Jung boldly proclaims the existence of an innate *spiritus rector*, writing,

> In spite of or perhaps because of its affinity with instinct, the archetype represents the authentic element of spirit, but a spirit which is not to be identified with the human intellect, since it is the latter's *spiritus rector*. The essential content of all mythologies and all religions…is archetypal (CW 8 ¶406).

Chapter 7

The Transcendent Function

I want to highlight some changes in my clinical practice since I began my endurance training. First, there have been several tangible changes. My practice has continued to grow, both in terms of patients I see for analysis as well as other aspects of my practice, such as forensic psychology. I feel much more confident as a clinician, as a student, and as an analyst-in-training. I have established several important professional relationships with other colleagues in our community that have served to generate many referrals.

In addition, recently the opportunity to purchase our group practice became available. As I considered my dreams and my recent experiences from my endurance training, I decided that I wanted to take on this new level of professional responsibility. The ownership has come with its own set of difficulties and challenges; I have tried to meet them with the same level of openness and psychic candor that I learned from my endurance training.

Finally, in purchasing our group practice, I relocated our offices and designed a new suite. In designing my new office, I separated my consulting room from my desk, phone, files, etc. with a half-wall. In sitting still, contemplating my thesis and looking over my consulting room, it became very clear to me the very deep, lasting value my numinous experiences have had on my clinical practice. Allow one example to suffice: Behind the couch that my analysands use is the half wall capped with a wooden mantel. On top of the wooden mantel, without consciously realizing it, I placed, in sequence, images and/or symbols mapping out the process of experiencing the transcendent function—what might be termed the transcendent function continuum.

For example, on the far-left side, I placed my statue of Shiva. As Joseph Campbell noted, Shiva is an image of the beginning/end, the everlasting dance of life, the divine child and the fire that is ever creating (cf., Campbell, 1949).

Next to Shiva, I placed a piece of stained glass depicting the Annunciation. I have long been moved by this biblical story and its images. I understand the Annunciation to be a story filled with images of insight, the spark, an impregnation, and a divine inkling that if followed, may turn out to be richly rewarded.

Next to the Annunciation, I placed my seated gargoyle. The gargoyle is representative of the seeming grotesque human body that the Divine inspiration finds itself. The fact that my gargoyle has large ears and a wry smile only serves to underscore the value of listening with open ears, despite the apparent ugliness of what is said or the seeming mundane world, knowing only too well that our humanness shades and distorts the Divine presence found everywhere.

Next to my seated gargoyle, I placed my stained glass piece depicting the birth of Christ. This piece is very special to me denoting that one has endured the darkness and longing of Advent and thus, has been made privy to the new idea, thought, feeling, and/or psychological presence promised by the Annunciation. A psychological birth has occurred in the most unlikely of places and I am then charged with the responsibility of its care.

Next, I placed my stained glass piece of the Holy Family's Flight into Egypt. This piece signifies to me the critical importance of trusting the dream, inkling, impregnation, no matter what, knowing there may be others who will sabotage or seek to kill the Divine presence. That is, it is not enough to have the dream, but one must equally work to protect it in its infancy and work to make manifest its value for one's life.

Finally, if one has been blessed with a psychological pregnancy, has been able to carry their psychological child to term, and has managed to steer clear of would be intruders, one is then in a position to feel the presence of the Holy Spirit, the Paraclete, and the *spiritus rector*. That is, my final piece is a replica of the Holy Spirit stained glass window from the National Cathedral in Washington, D.C. When listening to my analysands, I can often find myself orienting myself along this transcendent function continuum and thereby, helping to inform what I may say or offer.

Chapter 8

A Symbol of Renewal

As I began writing this material and began to imagine the daunting task of contemplating how I wanted to present my experiences, I had the following dream:

> *I was standing next to a skunk on a table—the skunk was on its back, splayed out, and fully awake and conscious, and subservient to a ritual. The very same woman from my "Isle People Water Dream" was present and approving of the ritual. She was sitting back in a chair, watching carefully, and nodding in approval. In the ritual I was to use my hand to scoop out the guts of the skunk and eat them. As I did this, the skunk transformed and became a divine/eternal child—also awake and alert, on its back and subservient to the ritual. I hesitated slightly but after being encouraged by the woman through her head nod and the look on her face, I scooped out of the guts and ate it. It was sweet, fruit-like. I awoke with a very warm feeling.*

Implicit throughout this material is the presence of my shadow. Whether exemplified as my penchant for order and certitude, my fear of my personal limitedness, my fear of the fluidity and intensity of affect, or at a very minimum, the ways in which I keep others at bay out of fear of not being accepted and my desire for deep introversion, this dream makes very clear to me: To realize one's deepest spiritual centers and thereby, one's inherent individuation, one must first assimilate/consume/digest one's own shadow. I was without a conscious relationship to Mercurius, a life-animating principle, when I entered analytic training. Living in my head and being fed by my thoughts, I was without relationship to my emotional centers. In a grand enantiodromia ushered in through my leave of absence and heralded by my synchronistic experiences in the Detroit marathon, I was continually taught in beautiful and loving ways how to be fed by recognizing my limitedness and personal shortcomings.

In my dream the skunk is splayed out, participating in a ritual, and I scooped out its guts and consumed them. What an apt image for assimilating my shadow—the skunk known for its instinct to keep its predators at bay with its anal scent glands when threatened. My reticence notwithstanding and by eating the skunk's guts, a transformation takes place, and a Divine child is born. Speaking to this psychic image, Jung wrote,

> The 'child' is born out of the womb of the unconscious, begotten out of the depths of human nature, or rather out of living Nature herself. It is a personification of vital forces quite outside the limited range of our conscious mind; of ways and possibilities of which our one-sided conscious mind knows nothing; a wholeness which embraces the very depths of Nature. It represents the strongest, the most

ineluctable urge in every being, namely the urge to realize itself. It is, as it were, an incarnation of the inability to do otherwise, equipped with all the powers of nature and instinct…The urge and compulsion to self-realization is a law of nature and thus of invincible power, even though its effect, at the start is insignificant and improbable. Its power is revealed in the miraculous deeds of the child hero…" (CW 9i ¶289).

That this dream draws particular attention to the fact that both the skunk and the Divine child are awake and alert and consciously participating in the ritual seems especially noteworthy. This is perhaps related to the fact that I was able to apprehend the symbols from my dreams and intuitions grounded in my body serving as an analytic vessel and then honor them through my endurance training—I was consciously participating in the ritual of life itself. To this end, Jung wrote,

> The symbols of the self arise in the depths of the body and they express its materiality every bit as much as the structure of the perceiving consciousness. The symbol is thus a living body, corpus et anima; hence the term 'child' is such an apt formula for the symbol. The uniqueness of the psyche can never enter wholly into reality, it can only be realized approximately, though it still remains the absolute basis of all consciousness (CW 9i ¶291).

Moreover, the fact that the dream image does not specifically identify a father is also remarkable (cf., CW 16 ¶ 378). This may well have to do with what Jung meant when he wrote that wisdom, born of the hard psychological work inherent in this process, serves as the father and thus represents a totality that transcends consciousness (CW 11 ¶221).

Jung thus has linked the image of the Divine Child with the individuation process leading to the birth of the mature adult and thereby expressing the inherent uniqueness of each individual. Finally, and not surprisingly, Jung also links the divine child specifically to the Self,

Lastly, the fact that I scoop out the guts and consume them seems also to be related to the feeling function. That is, far from the stereotypic locus of the thinking function, namely the head/brain, this dream image specifically highlights the guts, the stereotypic locus of the heart, the feelings, and one's emotional center. In short, in this dream, I am taught how to be fed by my feelings (CW 11 ¶755).

In summary then, this Divine child dream underscores the sacred ritual nature of my new-found sense of psychological agency, using my hands to scoop out and be fed by Nature herself. To do so, I first acknowledge and assimilate my own limitedness and personal darkness. Such an approach to life serves to transform life itself and bring about the birth of the Divine child, what Jung has identified as a "second Adam, God-man, Paraclete, a *complexio oppositorum*, the alpha and omega, the mediator and *intermedius*, as well as a *filius solis* et lunae" (CW 11 ¶713). The living experience of such an image and its psychological implications was for Jung akin to being in constant relationship with one's inherent *spiritus rector*. Or to put it differently, living in conscious communion with one's "urge to realize itself" brings about an experience of wholeness such that the sweet fruits of Nature herself become one's daily soul food.

I have demonstrated through description of my training for and participating in long distance endurance events evidence of Jung's model of individuation. I have laid particular emphasis on the role of the transcendent function through amplification of my dreams, fantasy and symbols, development of the inferior function, and finally the role of the archetype. I have offered evidence of how, in discovering the sacred ritual inherent in my training and competing in long distance endurance events, I have: learned to swim and live amongst the deep treasure bearing waters of Mercurius; to completely trust the egg bearing, patient presence promised in the worship song of the *anima*; to accept a loving trophy of Eros honoring all my experiences and teaching me to accept and treasure the love of those around me; to truly play amidst all of the apparent absurdities and seeming impossibilities of life and to daily renew my trust in my personal breath-soul; and finally, by doing so, how I am graced with the birth of my Divine child, a sacred experience of truly living Nature herself and of the ineluctable urge to wholly realize oneself. Thereby, I have offered evidence of the development of my relationship with the *spiritus rector* of Nature herself. Keep moving forward.

Epilogue

Following the completion of Ironman Wisconsin and the Chicago Ultra-Marathon, I continued to train for long distance endurance events and completed two more Ironman events as well as an Ultra-Ironman distance event and a second ultra-marathon. Each event brought with it the same numinous qualities. For instance, on the eve of Ironman Florida, I had a dream in which,

> *A Native American Indian dressed in spectacular clothing all knitted and outfitted in turquoise jewelry and beautiful ornate feathers, danced a ceremonial ritual dance while leading me through the whole Ironman Florida course.*

I awoke excited and ready for the day and earned my best Ironman finish time (11 hours and 57 minutes).

To close, I want to note one final dream. However, it is important to provide some context prior to relaying the dream. The first graduate courses I took in Analytical Psychology were taught at an 18th century Spanish Mission—Mission San Antonia De Padua in Jolon, California. The time at the Mission was to be spent largely in silence and meditative reflection. Later, a paper documenting our experiences would serve as a means for our grade. I instantly fell in love with the experience and had many foundational dreams while at the Mission.

A few nights prior to my graduation for my Diploma in Analytical Psychology, I had the following dream:

> *It is in the middle of the night and I am being led into a room that feels very ancient. I realize that a ritual is being enacted. The room has a very high, vaulted ceiling with oversized wooden beams that support its weight. Despite the darkness of the night, the room is brightly lit. After singing some ceremonial songs and chanting, I am led further into the room to witness the Craftsman at work. As my eyes adjust to the room, I can see the back of the Craftsman who is high on a ladder using his woodworking tools to spell the names of all psychoanalysts in an ornate calligraphy along one of the walls. I am then shown that he was in the process of completing mine. It is important to note that each name fit perfectly in a grand tapestry with one another. I began crying and the dream ended.*

Since completing the training to earn the Diploma of Analytical Psychology, I felt a deep need to reconnect with the professor that taught the courses at Mission San Antonio De Padua. With luck, I was able to speak with him and indicated that I wanted to show my gratitude to him and the Mission by attending as a guest during one of the courses—if they were still being held. Indeed, the courses were still being taught in the same manner, and I was very welcome to attend. However, once I arrived, I was given the honor of teaching several of the sessions—a thrill I will never forget. When the opportunity presented itself, I shared the Craftsman dream. The professor reminded me that the room in which all of the lectures take place used to be the "Craftsman's room," and the high beams, vaulted ceilings, etc., allowed for the work necessary to sustain the Mission to take place. I was, again, filled with tears of awe at the magnificence and genius of the dream.

References

The Holy Bible: Red Letter Edition, King James Version. 1994. Nashville, TN: Thomas Nelson Publishers,

Campbell, Joseph. 1949. *The Hero with a Thousand Faces.* New Jersey: Princeton University Press.

———. 1988. "The First Story Tellers," *Joseph Campbell and the Power of Myth*, Episode 3. Public Broadcasting System (PBS) Series (https://billmoyers.com/content/ep-3-joseph-campbell-and-the-power-of-myth-the-first-storytellers-audio/06/01/2020)

———. 1996. *Mythology and the Individual.* Joseph Campbell Audio Collection, Vol. 1. Audio Cassette.

Edinger, Edward. 1985. *Anatomy of the Psyche.* LaSalle: Open Court Publishing.

Guggenbühl-Craig, Adolph. 1980. *Eros on Crutches: Reflections on Psychopathy and Amorality.* Dallas: Spring Publications.

Hillman, James. 1985. Anima: An Anatomy of a Personified Notion. Dallas: Spring Publications.

James, Lynn. 2006. *Ironman Wisconsin Race Report.* 2006 Race Report to Triple Triathalon Team (n.p.)

Jung, C. G. *Collected Works*. eds. Read, Herbert, Michael Fordham, and Gerhard Adler, exec ed William McGuire. Princeton, NJ: Princeton University Press.

1911/1916. *Psychology of the Unconscious: A Study of the Transformations and Symbolisms of the Libido*, trans. Beatrice M. Hinkle. New York: Moffat, Yard and Company.

———. 1953. *Two Essays on Analytical Psychology*. Princeton: Princeton University Press.

———. 1965. *Memories, Dreams, Reflections,* Revised Edition, ed. Aniela Jaffe, trans. Richard and Clara Winston, New York: Vintage Books.

———. 1976. *The Visions Seminars* (Book Two), ed. Claire Douglas. Princeton: Princeton University Press.

Matthews, Boris L., trans. 1986. *The HerderDictionary of Symbols*: *Symbols from Art, Archaeology, Mythology, Literature, and Religion*. Wilmette, IL: Chiron Publications.

Winnicott, Donald. 1971. *Playing and Reality*. London: Routledge.

Index

A

affect 11, 13, 62
algae 24, 25, 26
Ambassador Bridge 3
analysis 23, 27, 34, 57
analytic training 6, 7, 8, 9, 10, 11, 19, 21, 23, 26, 28, 32, 38, 62
anima 12, 13, 39, 55, 63
anxiety 2, 3, 4, 17, 18, 30, 45
Aphrodite 40
athletes 17, 31, 33, 42, 43, 44, 45, 46

B

body 1, 4, 9, 11, 15, 18, 19, 21, 22, 24, 28, 30, 34, 37, 40, 43, 44, 45, 46, 48, 58, 63
breath 1, 3, 4, 11, 12, 13, 14, 15, 16, 17, 19, 21, 24, 25, 28, 31, 37, 55, 65
breathe 1, 2, 3, 4, 11, 21, 22, 55
breath soul 12, 25

C

calories 29, 30, 31, 41, 52, 53
Campbell, Joseph 6, 10, 17, 18, 34, 58, 71
Canada 3
Christ 10, 58
Christian 10
coach 18, 34, 42
collective unconscious 12
Columbus Marathon 28
conscious 8, 12, 13, 14, 18, 22, 61, 62, 64
control stage 7, 26
control supervision 23
cry 5, 40

D

death 10, 25, 47
Detroit 3, 5, 9, 12, 15, 17, 30, 47, 62
devil 12
diamond body 53
discipline 35, 36, 38, 51
divine 58, 61, 64
dream xi, 2, 4, 7, 9, 10, 11, 13, 14, 16, 17, 18, 19, 20, 21, 22, 24, 25, 26, 27, 30, 31, 38, 39, 40, 51, 52, 53, 54, 59, 61, 62, 63, 64, 67, 68

E

emotions 4, 11
endurance 6, 8, 19, 24, 28, 30, 31, 34, 55, 57, 63, 64, 67
endurance sports 6, 8, 28, 30, 55

F

feeling 2, 3, 4, 7, 9, 11, 13, 14, 25, 26, 27, 28, 30, 39, 40, 41, 42, 44, 51, 52, 53, 59, 61, 64
fish 24
Freedom Bridge 3, 4, 11

G

god 40

H

hero 6, 10, 13, 18, 63

I

imagination xiii
individuation 6, 8, 9, 12, 62, 63, 64
infinite 24, 48
institute xii
intuition 5, 9, 11
Ironman Wisconsin 32, 33, 35, 48, 67, 71
island people 1

J

journey 3, 6, 9, 10, 18, 35, 42, 46
Jung, C. G. xi, xiii, xiv, 6, 8, 9, 10, 11, 12, 19, 22 23, 42, 39, 40, 48, 53, 55, 62, 63, 64

L

lake 1, 10, 16, 17, 52

M

Madison, Wisconsin 38
marathon 2, 3, 4, 5, 9, 12, 15, 16, 17, 27, 28, 29, 30, 31, 32, 41, 45, 46, 47, 62
meditation 21, 22, 28
Mercurius 12, 13, 25, 62, 65
Mission San Antonia De Padua 67
monitoring committee 8
morning xi, 2, 3, 4, 22, 28, 29, 33, 34, 36, 42

N

Native American 67
nature xi, xii, 12, 13, 31, 36, 62, 64

night 4, 33, 46, 51, 68
numinous 5, 11, 19, 26, 34, 42, 58, 67
nutrition 19, 29, 42, 43, 44, 46, 47

P

play 51, 53, 54, 55, 65
prayer 5, 36, 38, 42
psychoanalysis xii, 19

R

rain 37, 42, 43, 44, 45, 46, 47, 52
rebirth 10, 11
renew 24, 26, 65
ritual 13, 14, 18, 19, 35, 36, 38, 55, 61, 62, 63, 64, 67, 68

S

self 10, 12, 49, 52, 54, 55, 63
shadow 62
ship 2, 13
Shiva 58
skunk 61, 62, 63
sky 1, 5
soul 4, 10, 12, 13, 14, 15, 17, 19, 21, 24, 28, 31, 37, 39, 48, 55, 64, 65
soul-making 39
spirit 4, 8, 24, 31, 34, 38, 39, 48, 55
spiritual knowledge 11
spiritus rector 6, 48, 53, 55, 64, 65
sprint triathlon 15, 16
subtle body 12
sun 1, 3, 5, 9, 10, 11, 22, 25
swimming 1, 11, 15, 16, 18, 20, 21, 22, 25, 33, 37, 40
synchronistic 11, 12, 62

T

taper 40
teacher 15
tears 2, 5, 47, 69

thinking 8, 11, 14, 30, 31, 43, 52, 64
training xii, 4, 6, 7, 8, 9, 15, 16, 18,
    19, 23, 24, 27, 28, 29, 30, 33, 34,
    35, 36, 38, 39, 40, 41, 42, 45, 46,
    51, 52, 57, 63, 64, 68
training case 7, 23
training schedule 18, 19
transcendent function 6, 8, 12, 14,
    38, 53, 55, 58, 59, 64
transformation 10, 11, 25, 40, 62
treasure xii, 2, 13, 14, 65
triathlete 18, 36
triathlon 15, 16, 17, 18, 21, 27, 32,
    35, 40, 41, 44, 47, 48, 51
triathlon club 18
trickster 12, 31
trophy 39, 40, 48, 53, 55, 65

U

ultra-marathon 51, 52, 53, 67
unconscious xiv, 8, 9, 12, 14, 17, 53,
    62

W

water 1, 2, 7, 9, 11, 13, 16, 18, 20, 21,
    22, 24, 25, 26, 30, 31, 32, 40, 42,
    43, 52, 55
white eggs 25, 26
wife 2, 5, 17, 29, 30, 41, 43, 45, 47,
    48, 52
William Blake xiv, 38
wind 3, 37, 43, 44, 45, 46, 47, 52, 53

About the Author

Warren W. Sibilla Jr., Ph.D. is a Clinical Psychologist and Diplomate Jungian Psychoanalyst who practices in South Bend, Indiana, USA.

In addition to his private practice, Dr. Sibilla has served in various leadership roles at the C. G. Jung Institute in Chicago, including serving as the Co-Director for the Jungian Psychotherapy Program for eight years and now as the Director-Elect of the Analyst Training Program.

He is currently writing a book on the relationship between Zen Buddhism and Analytical Psychology using the Ox Herding Pictures from 10th century China. Finally, he is most proud to say that he is a foster parent for rescued dogs in the community.